Mad about...
Sharks

written by Deborah Murrell
illustrated by Sue Hendra

consultants: the Shark Trust
www.sharktrust.org

A catalogue record for this book is available from the British Library

Published by Ladybird Books Ltd
80 Strand, London WC2R 0RL
A Penguin Company

016
© LADYBIRD BOOKS LTD MMVIII
LADYBIRD and the device of a Ladybird are trademarks of Ladybird Books Ltd

ISBN-13: 978-1-84646-798-1

Printed in China

Contents

Some words appear in **bold** in this book.
Turn to the glossary to learn about them.

What are sharks?

Sharks are fish. Most fish have hard **skeletons** made of bone, just like ours, but sharks have skeletons made of **cartilage**. This is lighter and more flexible than bone. We all have cartilage in the bendy part of our noses!

There are more than 450 types of sharks and they come in all shapes and sizes. This spinner shark has a long, powerful, **streamlined** body and sharp teeth.

If you have a computer, you can download a poster of different sharks from www.ladybird.com/madabout

Angel sharks are flat in shape. Their eyes are on top of their heads so they can see when they are lying on the bottom of the seabed.

Most sharks are less than two metres long and some, like this spined pygmy shark, are only about 25 centimetres long.

7

Older than the dinosaurs

There have been sharks swimming in our seas for about 400 million years, 200 million years before dinosaurs existed. Most early sharks were only a metre or two long. Unfortunately, sharks' skeletons do not make very good fossils, so we do not know very much about them.

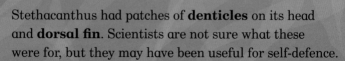

Stethacanthus had patches of **denticles** on its head and **dorsal fin**. Scientists are not sure what these were for, but they may have been useful for self-defence.

Xenacanthus was a freshwater shark that died out about 260 million years ago. Its long dorsal fin makes it look a bit like an eel.

dorsal fin

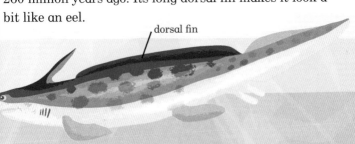

Megalodon was a meat-eating shark that probably died out about one and a half million years ago. It would have been 12-15 metres long, two or three times the size of a great white shark. Fossils of its teeth have been found that are up to 17 centimetres long – about the size of a human hand!

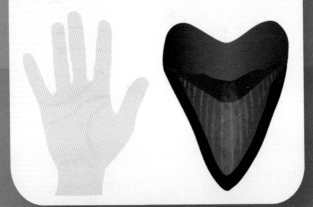

Sharks' bodies

Sharks' bodies are perfectly made for living in water. They have special ways of breathing, eating and swimming that have helped them survive for millions of years.

Dorsal fin to help keep the shark upright and stable in the water

Strong tail to power the shark through the water

Sharks have good eyesight, but their senses of hearing and smell are even better. They can hear sounds up to one and a half kilometres away. Some sharks can also smell blood in the water up to 400 metres away!

A shark's skin is made from **dermal denticles**. When it is rubbed from back to front, it is so rough that people once used it as sandpaper!

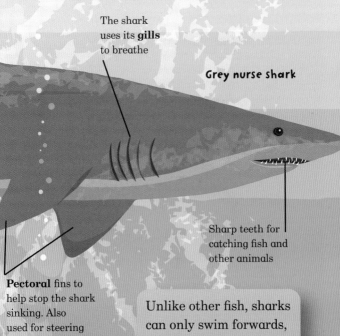

The shark uses its **gills** to breathe

Grey nurse shark

Sharp teeth for catching fish and other animals

Pectoral fins to help stop the shark sinking. Also used for steering

Unlike other fish, sharks can only swim forwards, not backwards.

11

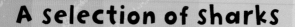

A selection of sharks

The great white
shark is probably the
best known of all sharks.
It is the largest of the **predator**
sharks, and can be over six metres long.

Young lemon sharks
sometimes behave in a
threatening way to divers,
but adults are very timid.

Blue sharks are dark
blue on top and light blue
underneath. This makes them difficult to
see both from the surface and under the water.

Basking sharks are large sharks that often swim near the ocean surface. They feed by gulping in water that contains tiny sea creatures.

Leopard sharks are easily recognized by their dark spots. They are large, but harmless to people.

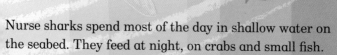

Nurse sharks spend most of the day in shallow water on the seabed. They feed at night, on crabs and small fish.

The weird and wonderful!

Some sharks have strange and interesting features. In some cases it is obvious how a feature is useful, and helps the shark to survive. In others, scientists simply do not know.

Cookiecutter sharks get their name from the round shapes they bite out of larger animals, such as seals.

round cookiecutter bites

Goblin sharks live in the darkest depths of the ocean. They have existed for seventy million years but scientists thought they were **extinct** until some were found near Japan about one hundred years ago.

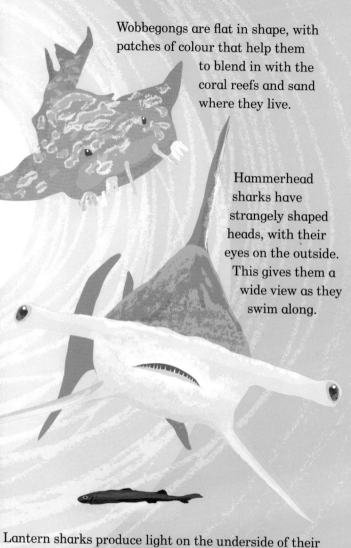

Wobbegongs are flat in shape, with patches of colour that help them to blend in with the coral reefs and sand where they live.

Hammerhead sharks have strangely shaped heads, with their eyes on the outside. This gives them a wide view as they swim along.

Lantern sharks produce light on the underside of their bodies. They live in deep Atlantic waters and the light may attract food, such as squid and crab, in the dark.

15

Where are they?

Sharks live in oceans all over the world. They are most common in warm water, though a few live as far north as the Arctic Ocean. Some sharks travel great distances, while others spend their entire lives in a small area.

●	●	●	●
Greenland shark	Wobbegong	Nurse shark	Mako shark

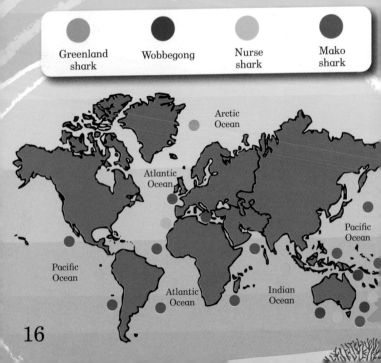

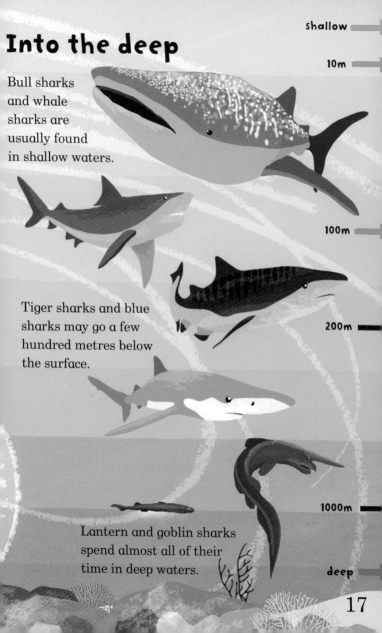

Into the deep

Bull sharks
and whale
sharks are
usually found
in shallow waters.

Tiger sharks and blue
sharks may go a few
hundred metres below
the surface.

Lantern and goblin sharks
spend almost all of their
time in deep waters.

Shallow

10m

100m

200m

1000m

deep

17

Feeding time!

Most sharks are predators and actively hunt for food. Only the whale shark, basking shark and megamouth shark feed by constantly grazing on small sea creatures. This is called filter-feeding.

pores

Hammerheads like to feed on stingrays. The sting does not seem to put them off! They have special **pores** on the underside of their heads that can sense the electric currents of stingrays hidden in the sand.

Megamouth is a rare type of shark that was not discovered until 1976. It feeds mainly on **krill**, and has huge lips that glow in the dark. Scientists think this may lure krill into its mouth.

lips

Tiger sharks' teeth are multi-purpose. The sharp point bites into **prey**, and the **serrated** edge cuts it up. The teeth are strong enough to crunch through a turtle's shell and bones.

Port Jackson sharks eat animals that live on the ocean floor, such as crabs. They have sharp front teeth for catching and holding prey and strong, flat back teeth that can crunch up hard shells.

Nurse sharks have soft mouths, which they use for finding and sucking up food from the sea floor.

The great white shark can eat a whole sea lion in one go! Scientists think that after a large meal, the great white can go without eating for up to three months.

Shark babies

Most sharks give birth to live babies, called pups, but others lay eggs. Once the baby sharks are born or hatch, they must fend for themselves if they are to survive.

Swell shark eggs
The mother lays eggs protected in special egg cases. These hatch outside the mother, just like birds or other fish.

Horn shark eggs
These egg cases are a funny spiral shape and take around six to nine months to hatch.

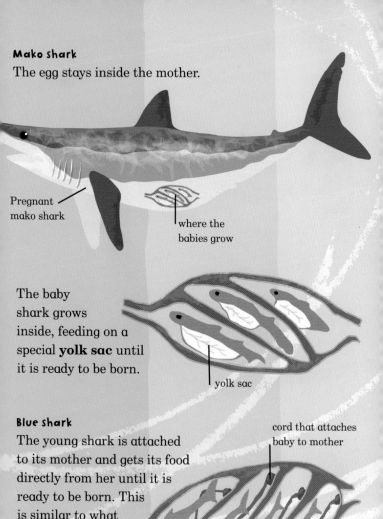

Mako shark
The egg stays inside the mother.

Pregnant
mako shark

where the
babies grow

The baby
shark grows
inside, feeding on a
special **yolk sac** until
it is ready to be born.

yolk sac

Blue shark
The young shark is attached
to its mother and gets its food
directly her until it is
ready to be born. This
is similar to what
happens with
many **mammals**,
including people.

cord that attaches
baby to mother

21

Sharks and people

Some people think of sharks as dangerous, man-eating monsters. However, the truth is very different. Fewer than 80 shark attacks on people are recorded each year and very few people (usually between three and six) are killed.

Most shark attacks are the result of people annoying sharks,

Can you tell what these things are?

or mistaken identity. Seals, turtles and a person on a surfboard look very alike from underwater. Sharks may also smell blood from wounds and come to investigate. Often, once a shark discovers its mistake, it lets go and the person can swim to safety.

People who swim with sharks usually take good care of their safety. They may wear protective clothing or dive in a cage, especially if they are filming the shark. Cages protect the valuable equipment as well as the person!

Great white shark

Four of the sharks most likely to attack people are:
• bull shark
• great white shark
• tiger shark
• oceanic white tip

23

Fantastic factfile

- Most sharks live only in the salty oceans, but bull sharks have often been found in freshwater rivers and lakes in North and South America.

- In parts of Africa, the shark is considered sacred. If a shark is killed by accident, special rituals must be performed to make up for its death.

- The egg cases of some sharks are sometimes called 'mermaid's purses'.

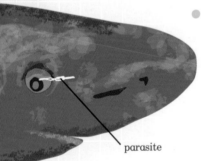

parasite

- Tiny **parasites** attach themselves to the eyes of Greenland sharks and can make them partly blind. Some scientists think that the parasites dangling from the sharks' eyes may attract smaller fish, which the sharks then snap up!

- Sharks never run out of teeth. New rows of teeth are constantly being formed in their mouths. If one tooth is lost or worn out, another one moves forward to replace it.

- The basking shark filters half a million litres of seawater through its mouth every hour.

- Most fish have just one gill slit for breathing on each side of their bodies, but sharks can have up to seven on each side.

gills

- When swell sharks are threatened, they wedge themselves into a crack or gap in a rock and gulp in mouthfuls of water to make their bodies look bigger and scarier!

- Atlantic blue sharks travel around the ocean in a circuit each year, covering about 25,000 kilometres on the way.

- More people are killed each year by dogs and pigs than by sharks!

25

Amazing shark awards

⭐ Fastest

The shortfin mako can swim at speeds of up to 72 kilometres per hour. That's about as fast as a racehorse on land.

⭐ Strongest bite

A dusky shark applies 60 kilograms of pressure per tooth on its prey. That's like being crushed beneath the weight of ten cars!

⭐ Biggest

The whale shark is the largest living fish. It can grow up to 14 metres long and weigh 15 tonnes. That's as heavy as two African elephants.

Smallest

The smallest shark so far found is the dwarf lantern fish. Fully grown males can measure as little as 16 centimetres, which is about the length of a pen.

Most dangerous

The great white is responsible for more attacks on humans than any other **species** of shark. Even so, in an average year only six or seven attacks are recorded.

Highest jump

The shortfin mako shark often leaps up to six metres above the water – that's more than three times the height of an average adult!

Save the shark!

People have hunted sharks for many years. Today however, overfishing is threatening many sharks' existence, and other problems, such as the loss of their **habitats**, could also cause some kinds to become extinct.

In many places where people used to hunt sharks, they now take visitors on trips to watch sharks in their natural habitat.

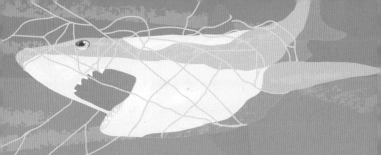

Sharks are often caught in fishing nets. Many die because they cannot move in order to breathe.

In some countries, sharks are caught and killed to make shark fin soup. Shark meat is also eaten all round the world.

Shark fins

SHARK FIN

SOUP

What can we do?

We can join **conservation** groups that work to help save sharks and their ocean homes. Learning about sharks and telling others how amazing they are may also encourage people to help save them.

Glossary

cartilage – a firm but bendy material from which sharks' skeletons are made.

conservation – the protection of nature, animals and plants.

denticle – small tooth or a tooth-like growth.

dermal denticles – tiny tooth-like scales that cover a shark's body.

dorsal – on or relating to the upper side or back.

extinct – an animal or plant that no longer exists.

fin – part of the body of a shark used for swimming, steering or balancing.

gills – parts of an animal used for breathing under water.

habitat – the natural home of an animal or plant.

krill – a small, shrimp-like animal eaten by some sharks.

mammal – animal with a backbone and hair or fur, that gives birth to live young.

parasite – an animal that lives on and feeds from another animal or plant.

pectoral – on or relating to the chest.

pore – a small opening in the skin or other surface.

predator – animal that hunts and eats other animals.

prey – animals that are eaten by other animals.

serrated – jagged, like a saw's edge.

skeleton – a framework of bone or cartilage that gives an animal its shape.

species – a group of animals that look the same and can mate to have young.

streamlined – a long, slim shape that can move easily through water and air.

yolk sac – a pouch containing special food that feeds some baby animals until they are born.